The One Lettered Mantra of Rama
for
Rama Jayam - Likhita Japam Mala

Journal for Writing the One-Lettered Rama Mantra

एक अक्षर राम मंत्र

व

राम जयम - लिखित जपम

राम-नाम लेखन माला

Belongs to _____

Published by: **Rama-Nama Journals**
(an Imprint of e1i1 Corporation)

Title: **The One Lettered Mantra of Rama for Rama Jayam - Likhita Japam Mala**
Sub-Title: Journal for Writing the One-Lettered Rama Mantra

Author: **Sushma**

Copyright Notice: **Copyright © e1i1 Corporation © Sushma**
All rights reserved. No part of this publication may be reproduced, distributed, or transmitted in any form or by any means, including photocopying, recording, or other electronic or mechanical methods.

<u>Identifiers</u>
ISBN: **978-1-945739-31-6** (Paperback)

—o—

www.**e1i1**.com -- www.**OnlyRama**.com
email: **e1i1***books***e1i1**@gmail.com

Our books can be bought online, or at Amazon, or any bookstore. If a book is not available at your neighborhood bookstore they will be happy to order it for you. (Certain Hardcover Editions may not be immediately available—we apologize)

Some of our Current/Forthcoming Books are listed below. Please note that this is a partial list and that we are continually adding new books.
Please visit www.**e1i1**.com / www.**onlyRama**.com for current offerings.

- **Tulsi Ramayana—The Hindu Bible:** Ramcharitmanas with English Translation & Transliteration
- **Tulsi-Ramayana Rama-Nama Mala (multiple volumes):** Legacy Journals for Writing the Rama Name alongside Tulsidas Ramcharitmanas—contains English Translation & Transliteration, Inspirational Quotes of Hindu saints, and space for you to jot down your spiritual sentiments on a daily basis. Once embellished with your Rama-Namas, these books become priceless treasures which you can present to your loved ones—a true gift of love, labor, caring, wishing, and above all—Devotion.
- **Ramcharitmanas:** Ramayana of Tulsidas with Transliteration (in English)
- **Ramayana, Large**: Tulsi Ramcharitmanas, Hindi only Edition, Large Font and Paper size
- **Ramayana, Medium**: Tulsi Ramcharitmanas, Hindi only Edition, Medium Font and Paper size
- **Ramayana, Small**: Tulsi Ramcharitmanas, Hindi only Edition, Small Font and Paper size
- **Sundarakanda:** The Fifth-Ascent of Tulsi Ramayana
- **RAMA GOD:** In the Beginning - Upanishad Vidya (Know Thyself)
- **Purling Shadows:** And A Dream Called Life - Upanishad Vidya (Know Thyself)
- **Fiery Circle:** Upanishad Vidya (Know Thyself)
- **Rama Hymns:** Hanumān-Chalisa, Rama-Raksha-Stotra, Bhushumdi-Ramayana, Nama-Ramayanam, Rama-Shata-Nama-Stotra, etc. with Transliteration & English Translation
- **Rama Jayam - Likhita Japam Mala alongside Sacred Hindu Texts (several):** Journals for Writing the Rama Name 100,000 Times alongside various Hindu Texts, with English Translation & Transliteration. Embellish these Books with your Rama-Namas and they become transformed into priceless treasures which you can later gift to your loved ones.
- **Rama Jayam - Likhita Japam Mala alongside Rama-Mantras (several):** Journals for Writing the Rama Name alongside the Rama-Mantras from one lettered to thirty-two & others. Embellish these with your Rama-Namas and they become transformed into priceless treasures.

-- On our website may be found links to renditions of Rama Hymns --
-- Rama Mantras/Hymns/Pictures are also available printed on Quality Shirts from Amazon. See our website for details --

rāma-nāma mahimā

As per *Hindu-Darshan* (philosophy), there is just a one-Consciousness which pervades the Universe, with nothing else besides; and the very nature of that consciousness is Bliss. And yet, though our essential nature is rooted in Bliss, still most of us live in misery. Why? Well, according to Tulsidās, a gemstone is not valued until it is identified by its name. In the same way, the one immortal, true, sentient, complete, and blissful all-pervading Brahmm—persists in bondage and suffering (as the visible woeful creation), until becoming revealed into a definite form and name—energized by the Name 'Rāma'.

Rāma is Bliss. The Rāma-Nāma—Name of Rāma, is the key to that Bliss.

The potency of Rāma-Nāma is unsurpassed in all the four Yugas; the Vedas and other scriptures sing of its glories; and the saints swear by it—especially so in the present Age. In the Kali-Yuga, the chanting of Rāma-Nāma is regarded as most-effective and most-supreme—being that in such iniquitous Times, there is no other easy means of salvation.

The present Kali-Yuga, the Iron-Age, is rightly described as vile and sinful. It is awash with the six Gunas of Māyā: Kāma (Lust), Krodha (Anger), Lobha (Greed), Moha (Infatuation), Mada (Pride) & Mātsarya (Envy)—and here we find our minds sinking in worldliness despite our best intentions. Seemingly none can remain unsullied from the taints of Kali—this appears to be the fait-accompli of the Kali-Yuga—a very sad state indeed. But despair not, for when it comes to attaining salvation, many consider this Kali-Yuga to be the Golden-Age. Yes, Kali-Yuga has this one great blessing: through a very simple expediency—simply by a complete surrender to the Holy Name Rāma—one is able to attain to that very high divine state, that very supreme seat, which sages scarcely attained to even after practicing great penances and sacrifices in former Times.

In the Sata-Yuga, contemplation; in the Tretā, Sacrifice; and in the Dwāpar-Yuga worship—these were the appointed propitiations; but in this vile and impure Kali-Yuga—where the soul of man is like unto a fish floating in the ocean of sin—in such dreadful times, the Nāma is the only tree of eternal life; and by meditating upon it all the vile commotions become stilled. In these Times neither good deeds, nor piety, nor spiritual wisdom is of any avail—but only the Name of Rāma. The Rāma-Nāma is, as it were, the wisdom and might of Hanumān that exposes and destroys the Kālnemī-like wiles of the wicked world.

Sing the praises of the Lord and remain engaged in Nāma-Smarana—is the advice given to us by our saints; the Japa of Rāma-Nāma is the supreme path to salvation—assure our Scriptures; there is no Dharma higher than Nāma-Dharma in this Age—aver the wise. The chanting of Rāma-Nāma is The-One-Supreme-Path to escape the clutches of Kali-Yuga—declares Rāmacharitmānas; in fact it is the one and only Dharma which is easy and feasible given the vicious nature of the present Times.

Well do our scriptures repeatedly assert: In this Kali-Yuga, there is no other means, no other means, no other means of salvation—other than chanting the holy name Rāma, chanting the holy name Rāma, chanting the holy name Rāma.

Talking of the Rāma-Nāma, Tulsidās says: रा , म are the two most gracious syllables, the eyes as it were of the soul, the miracle charms which satisfy one's every wish, a gain for this world and felicity in the next. These are nectar-like syllables which abide together inseparably, and are most delightful to utter and hear, and easy to remember. Love naturally gets stirred up as we speak these two mystic syllables: syllables which abide together as inseparably as Rāma and Lakshman, or like the duo Nārayana & Nara; syllables which are as intimately connected as the Universal-Soul and the individual-soul; syllables that are preservers of the world and redeemers of the elect; syllables that shine resplendent like two bright jewels on the ears of Bhakti—Beauteous Devotion; syllables that are pure and beneficent as the Sun and the Moon; syllables that are like sweetness and contentment—the inseparable attributes of ambrosia; syllables that are as inseparable as the hovering bee of devout-souls to the lotus of the Supreme-Soul.

Yogis—who are full of dispassion and detached from the world—are able to keep awake in the daylight of wisdom repeating these two syllables of the Name of Rāma, and thus enjoy the incomparable felicity of Brahmm-Rāma—who is incomparable, unspeakable, unmixed with sorrow and void of name and form. *Gyanis*—those who aspire for knowledge—are able to understand all the mysteries by repeating the Name Rāma. *Sadhaks* (Strivers), who repeat the Name Rāma, absorbed in contemplation, become workers of miracles and acquire great mystic powers. They who repeat it when burdened with affliction are freed from their troubles and become blissful and content.

There are four kinds of devotees, and all the four are virtuous, sinless, and noble, and all the four—clever as they are—rely upon the Rāma Name. Even those—who are free from all desires and remain ever absorbed in the joy of devotion to Shrī Rāma—throw their heart as fish into the nectarine lake of affection for the Name Rāma.

In all the four ages; in all times, past, present, or future; in the three spheres of earth, heaven and hell—any creature that repeats the name Rāma becomes blessed. The name of Rāma is like the tree of paradise, the centre of all that is good in the world; and whoever meditates upon it verily becomes transformed—from the vile to holy.

As Narasingh was manifested to destroy Hiranyā-kashyap, the enemy of heaven—in order to protect Prahlād—so is the Name of Rāma for the destruction of the wicked and the protection of the pious.

The chanting of Rāma-Nāma is a direct way to liberation. By repeating this name—whether in joy or in sadness, in activity or in repose—bliss is diffused all around. According to the Vedas, just as the sun dispels the darkness, the chanting of Rāma-Nāma dispels all the evils and obstacles of life. The Rāma Nāma cures agony and showers the blessings of God; all righteous wishes get fulfilled; jealousy and pride disappear; life becomes imbued with satisfaction and peace; all of life's needs fall in place automatically—just like a miracle of nature guiding nature's forces. You may not always get what you want in the exact same form, but the Rāma-Nāma will purify things and bring to you the same needed happiness and bliss in a much more refined and lasting way. Life truly becomes filled with tranquility. With the Rāma-Nāma, an immense sense of spiritual wellbeing is experienced apart from a gain of material happiness.

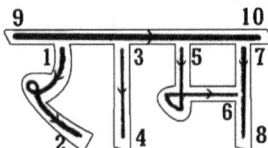

*If you do not know how to write राम in Sanskrit it is quite easy. Trace the contours 1-2 (which is the sound of **r** in '**r**un'), 3-4 (the sound of **a** in '**a**rk'), 5-6 & 7-8 (the sound **m** in '**m**ust') and lastly make the line 9-10.*

Rāma-Japa—the constant repetition of the Supreme-Mantra 'Rāma'—is usually done mentally, or on a rosary; but there is one extremely efficacious method of this Japa: the *Likhita-Japa*, or the Written-Chant. The practice of writing the Rāma Mantra over and over on paper is called the Likhita-Japa. This written form of Japa is a lasting record of your chant, remaining ever imbued with those holy vibrations, for all times, for the benefit of you and the future generations. In India, as you may know, devotees of God have been chanting the name 'Rāma' and writing the Name 'Rāma'—pages upon pages of it, running into billions and billions, for ages. Hindu children are taught to write the Rāma-Nāma from their very childhood.

The Likhita Rāma-Nāma Japa is a powerful and transformative tool. As you write the Rāma-Nāma, all the senses become engaged in the service of the Lord-God, and you find yourself simultaneously chanting and hearing and contemplating on the Lord—everything comes together naturally. This method clears away your thoughts and helps concentrate the entirety of your soul upon the Divine.

Any Japa is beneficial but somehow writing the Rāma-Nāma on paper brings up a great singularity of focus within the mind—and the peace of heart which ensues is something which is not so easily achieved with other forms of Japa. The written form of Rāma-Japa is somehow able to engage those parts of our body-mind continuum which other methods can not—and our meditative stance is able to gain much deeper levels thereby.

Although the Rāma-Mantra is the gateway to higher consciousness and spiritual upliftment, but even at such junctures—when you find yourself in odd situations, where all the paths seem blocked—then just walking away from everything and simply writing the Rāma Nāma, will give you a much needed clarity of thought—and a divine inspiration that will show a way out.

The Rāma Nāma is very transformative: with it you gain a balanced progress in your outside world and the inner. Sant Tulsidās says in Rāmacharitmānas: Place the Rāma-Nāma Jewel at the threshold, and there will be light both inside and out; i.e. a constant chant of the Rāma-Nāma from the mouth—the doorway to the body—will bring you external materialistic wellbeing, and also an inner spiritual wellness—both. Incredibly, with the Rāma-Nāma, you get to have the best of both the worlds.

There is something special that happens when you write the Rāma-Nāma. Peace and tranquility surrounds you as you write the Supreme-Mantra. The Rāma-Mantra imparts to you divine strength and great tolerance to withstand the vicissitudes of life. Bright unclouded wisdom illumines your mind. You find yourself in complete surrender to your inner Being. The resonance of God resonates throughout your mind-body continuity. You feel a flux of divine energy resonating within. You get great power and peace in your everyday life. The Japa of Rāma Mantra protects our inner world as well as the outside.

These journals are for doing the written-Japa of the Rāma-Mantras. Please note that at certain places in the Rāma-Rahasya Upanishad, it is advised to do a certain number of Chants following a prescribed method when trying to pursue a special objective—and you are welcome to follow that regimen if you so desire; however the focus of this journal is very simple: a simple introduction to the Mantra, and doing a Written-Japa of that Mantra to gain the grace of Lord Shri Rāma. Rāma is the most gracious forms of the Lord-God, and He gets pleased through the simplest of means.

This journal is for writing the Rāma-Mantra of One-Letter. A brief introduction of the Mantra is given and it is repeated on every page so you can replicate it. A larger Mantra outlines is also printed on each page for you to create a design as you write. If you fill this with the Rāma-Mantras using color/size/slant that is different from the outside—then it will also make a large Mantra stand out in the waves of surrounding Rāma-Mantras. Devotees usually make such interesting patterns in their Likhita Japa. Most Devotees will use red ink for writing; some will use different colors to create patterns; some will keep a special set of pens kept purely for the Likhita in the belief that such implements—that are habitually used for holy tasks—build up energy and holy resonance of their own. There are no hard rules; do what feels natural. Also, please feel free to choose any notebook or paper to write upon, not necessarily this Journal.

Write the Rāma-Mantra with reverence, every day, preferably at a set time, or as and when possible, in small measures, or copiously—howsoever your situation permits. There are no hard rules, do what feels good to your Soul. The important thing is to engage in the Likhita-Japa. When completed, you could keep the Likhita-Japas in your Worship-Room, preserve them as treasures to pass on to future generations, donate them to Rāma Temples, or gift them to your loved ones—who will thereby inculcate crucial values from you, and learn the importance of the Rāma-Nāma, and get inspired with Hindu Values, especially so the younger ones.

While writing, focus your mind on the Rāma-Mantra and chant it within. Imagine Sītā-Rāma showering you with their bliss. Try to stay free of distractions, and with time you will find that your mind will take a natural meditative stance while engaged in the written Rāma-Nāma Japa.

Once embellished with your Rāma-Nāmas, these Journals will become priceless treasures which you can present to your loved ones—an unparalleled gift of love, labor, caring, wishing, and above all—Devotion. We wish you a very blissful Rāma-Nāma Japam.

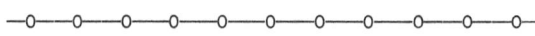

Our following Journals:
Tulsi-Ramayana Rama-Nama Mala (in multiple volumes): Legacy Journals for Writing the Rama Name alongside Full Tulsi Ramayana, are legacy Journals in which you can write down your spiritual sentiments, and the Rāma-Nāma, alongside the printed Tulsi Rāmayana. These Journal-Books contain the original text, transliteration, translation, and space for you to jot down your thoughts and write the Rāma-Nāma. Pages also have inspirational words of Hindu Saint to help guide aspirants on their spiritual journey. You can embellish the entire Tulsi Rāmayana with your Rāma-Nāmas and gift them to your loved ones—a truly unique gift of love, care, labor, and devotion.

Our following Journals:
Rama Jayam - Likhita Japam Mala alongside Sacred Hindu Texts (several)
are Journals for performing the 100,000 Rama-Nama Likhita Japa alongside Sacred Hindu Texts like:
Hanumān Chalisa, Nama Ramayanam, Rama-Ashtottara-Shata-Nama-Valih, Rama-Ashtottara-Shata-Nama-Stotra, Rama Raksha Stotra, Ramashtakam... *(and more on the way)*

the one-lettered mantra of śrī-rāma

Once, the enlightened *Rishis*: Mudgala, Shandilya, Paingala, Bikshu etc.—all distinguished seers who were skilled in philosophy and science, prodigious masters of austerities & penance—accompanied by other ascetics and sages like the Sanaka, as well as many devotees of Lord Vishnu such as Prahalād—approached Shri Hanumān.

These great masters—who had attained to the pinnacle of their spiritual knowledge and were considered most wise and erudite—had come to Hanumān in order to get access to the highest knowledge; and they said unto Hanumān: "O thou mighty brave Lord; O son-of-the-wind-god, do please teach us: What is that ultimate essence which is known to those who are renowned experts in the knowledge pertaining to Brahmm? What is the basis tenet, the cardinal essence, the substantive edict of the eighteen Puranas, the eighteen sub-Puranas, and the Smritis? The four Vedas and all the scriptures are well known to thee—they have been taught to thee by none other than the sun-god. Thy knowledge is more comprehensive than that of anyone. Oh the valiant brave Hanumān, do please tell: What is the essence of all the great teachings? What is the fundamental knowledge expounded and enunciated by the scriptures?"

And Hanumān replied: "O ye exalted sages, seers, ascetics, and devotees of the Lord! Listen carefully to what I have to say. It has the potential of destroying sin, and rent asunder all fetters of this deluding fearsome Creation. It incorporates the essence of all that's at the heart of our scriptures and metaphysics. The very core of the tenets, axioms and maxims, the greatest principle amongst them, is the principle of Tārak-Brahmm—that form of Brahmm which delivers one from the torments associated with this seemingly endless cycles of births and deaths; which releases the soul from bondages and into complete bliss and felicity. Hear ye all and know: It is Rāma who is the supreme transcendental Brahmm. Rāma is that ultimate *'Tattwa'*—the essence, the fundamental aspect—which thou enquire of and seek. It is Shri Rāma who is the Tārak Brahmm. Rāma is Brahmm personified, the embodiment of Supreme Consciousness & Bliss; Rāma is Para-Brahmm, the supreme austerity; Rāma is the Ultimate Essence of the Universe—the *Tārak-Brahmm*."

The sages enquired further and Hanumān detailed out to them the various aspects of the divine forms of Shri Rāma. Those great sages, led by Sanaka, now wished to learn of the Mantras for meditating upon Rāma and said, "Oh thou strong, valiant son of Anjani! Lord Rāma is celebrated as Tārak—the Redeemer, and as Brahmm—the All-Pervading Supreme-Soul. We request thee to please teach to us his Divine Holy Mantras for our welfare—those Mantras through which one can meditate and worship the Tārak-Brahmm Rāma." And Hanumān graciously taught to them the various Mantras of Rāma.

Of the many Mantras of Rāma, the very first one is the one-lettered Mantra of our Lord: रां (**rāṁ**)

This King of Mantras रां is called the Eka-ākshara Mantra—the one-syllabled.

This monosyllable is the *Beej* Mantra like the Om & others Seminal Mantras.

This Eka-ākshara Rāma रां is of the element of fire—the very treasure-house of energy. It is the seed from which all other divine Mantras of Rāma sprout from and develop into full-fledged Mantras.

This Eka-ākshara Rāma Mantra रां is the holistic representation of our divine Lord. It has the same import and value, the same mystical potencies and powers, as the *Kalpa-Vriksha*—the Heavenly-Tree which fulfills all the wishes of those who take the shelter under it.

This seed Mantra रां is a monosyllable sound, and it is represented in the written form as: the consonant र (r) with the vowel sound आ (ā) plus the consonant म (m)—both attached to it in the Matrā form. (In Sanskrit, आ (ā) in Matrā form is the vertical line; and म (m) in Matrā form is the dot at top.)

The sound of रां is like '*raaaaanggm*'—beginning with the '*ra*', followed by the extended sound '*aa*', and at the end the ringing '*nggm*': which is alike the background ethereal sound of the universe that reverberates throughout the Creation—and whose vibrations are heard in the *Nād* as well.

The invocation of this all-powerful, divine Mantra has the power to bestow upon the devotees all the benefits and blessings which they seek.

The *Rishi* (patron sage) of this रां Mantra is Brahamma, the Creator who first envisioned it. The *Chanda* (meter or poetic style) of this Mantra is the Gayatri. And the Lord-God Rāma Himself is the Devatā (the patron deity) of the Mantra रां.

This रां Mantra of the Lord Rāma is glorious and powerful and dynamic as the fire. Of the five elements (earth-water-air-fire-space), the resplendency and powers of Fire-element are inherently built within रां.

Verily रां is a store-house of fire: it has its roots in र 'r', which is the seed of fire-element; the long vowel आ 'A' implies the infinite, and has the effect of amplifying the fire element's powers; the म (Matrā-dot) on the top—alike the crown jewel imparting the Mantra its divine authority and sanctity—is representative of the beginning of Creation: coiled up and undefined. It represents the cosmic seed from which this entire Creation has unfolded. Just like a seed brings forth a new generation, likewise this *Beej* Mantra of the Lord-God has similar powers & dynamism. It fulfills all the wishes that are in the mind of the seeker.

An aspirant, who is desirous of receiving the blessings of Shri Rāma with a view to attaining complete liberation, should visualize the divine form of the Lord-God within the heart as follows:

[Dhyāna—Meditation]

On the north of the city of Ayodhyā, near the banks of the holy river Saryu, under a Mandar Tree, exists a magnificent pulpit, upon which is a lotus-like throne.

Lord-God Rāma—of a splendorous dark hue—is seated thereupon sporting the posture (*Virāsan*) of the bravest Hero, and with His arms holding the *Gyana Mudrā*—imparting knowledge.

The Lord's left hand rests on his left knee.

Shri-Sitā—the divine consort of the Lord, and **Shri Lakhman,** are by His side.

Bhagwān Shri-Rāma is immaculate, unsullied, divine & holy; radiant & self-resplendent alike a pure crystal; glowing with a self-generated divine hue of immense intensity that effuses out of His body.

With a benign smile, **Bhagwān Shri-Rāma** is looking directly at me with most benefaction.

[Dhyāna concludes]

An aspirant who is desirous of '*Moksha*'—total emancipation, complete liberation and deliverance of the Self—should meditate upon the Lord thusly, while doing the Japa of the holy divine Eka-ākshara Mantra twelve *lakh* times.

The devotee aspirant should meditate upon the Eka-ākshara Divine Mantra of Shri Rāma as being the personification of the Paramātma, the Supreme-Soul, who is more glorious and splendorous than a million suns.

Note:

Virāsan: A Yogic posture with one sitting atop their right leg. Both legs are bent at knees (fully); right leg is somewhat parallel to the ground, with only the toes touching the ground—the sole raised; the left leg is kind of vertical, with the entire sole touching the ground. The body is balanced only on the toe of right leg and the flat sole of left.

Gyana Mudrā: right hand—tips of index finger & thumb are touching, forming a ring; other three fingers held straight.

Lakh: Number 100,000.

obeisance to śrī-rāma

Obeisance to the Holy Being **Bhagwān Shri Rāmachandra**, Lord-God Incarnate, who is the Supreme-Absolute, the deification of eternal Bliss & pure Beatitude.

When the great Lord Vishnu, who is 'Sat-Chit-Ānand' embodied—absolute Truth, untainted Consciousness, untarnished Bliss—took birth as an Incarnation in the household of King Dasharath, in the lineage of Raghus, He was known by the name of **Shri Rāma**.

Rāma is none other than Mahā-Vishnu, the Supreme Being who manifested Himself upon Earth as an Avatār, who dwells to sport with His devotees, who fulfills their every desire.

The Lord is *'Swayambhu'*—self-born. He requires no external medium or cause to reveal himself in visible form; He has no one from whom He is born; He is eternal, without an end; He is ever present; He never dies. It is only when He makes himself physically manifest that creates the illusion of the Lord having taken birth or coming into being. His vanishing from sight—when He so desires, when His enactments in visible form on earth are completed—is regarded by the world as the Lord-God having left the earth for His heavenly abode.

In truth there is no going anywhere, nor a coming from anywhere for the Lord-God—being that Lord Rāma is the eternal, imperishable, omnipresent, immutable, Universal Constant. He reveals Himself without any cause whatsoever, requiring no reason to do so—for He does it out of His own sweet will, whenever He so deems fit, whenever it becomes to Him necessary and proper.

Lord Rāma is *Anant*—without an end, without a beginning; He is eternal and infinite; He has no measurable dimensions or attributes.

Lord Rāma is *Swayamev Bhāsatey*—He shines of his own self-effulgence; He makes His presence evident by itself, requiring no other proofs to establish His authenticity and veracity.

Lord Rāma is *Jyotirmaya*—the embodiment of light. He is the cosmic Consciousness which is self-illuminated, requiring no other source of light to illuminate or make His presence known.

Lord Rāma pervades throughout the Creation as the One-Consciousness. It is He—in the form of the indwelling consciousness—which resides in you and me, and in all beings & things. It is He who established this Creation and supports it.

Beyond the limiting confines of time, space, matter, **Rāma** is that pure consciousness which is eternally radiant but is indefinable, unqualified, attribute-less, immeasurable.

रं रं रं रं रं रं रं रं रं रं रं रं रं रं रं रं रं रं रं रं

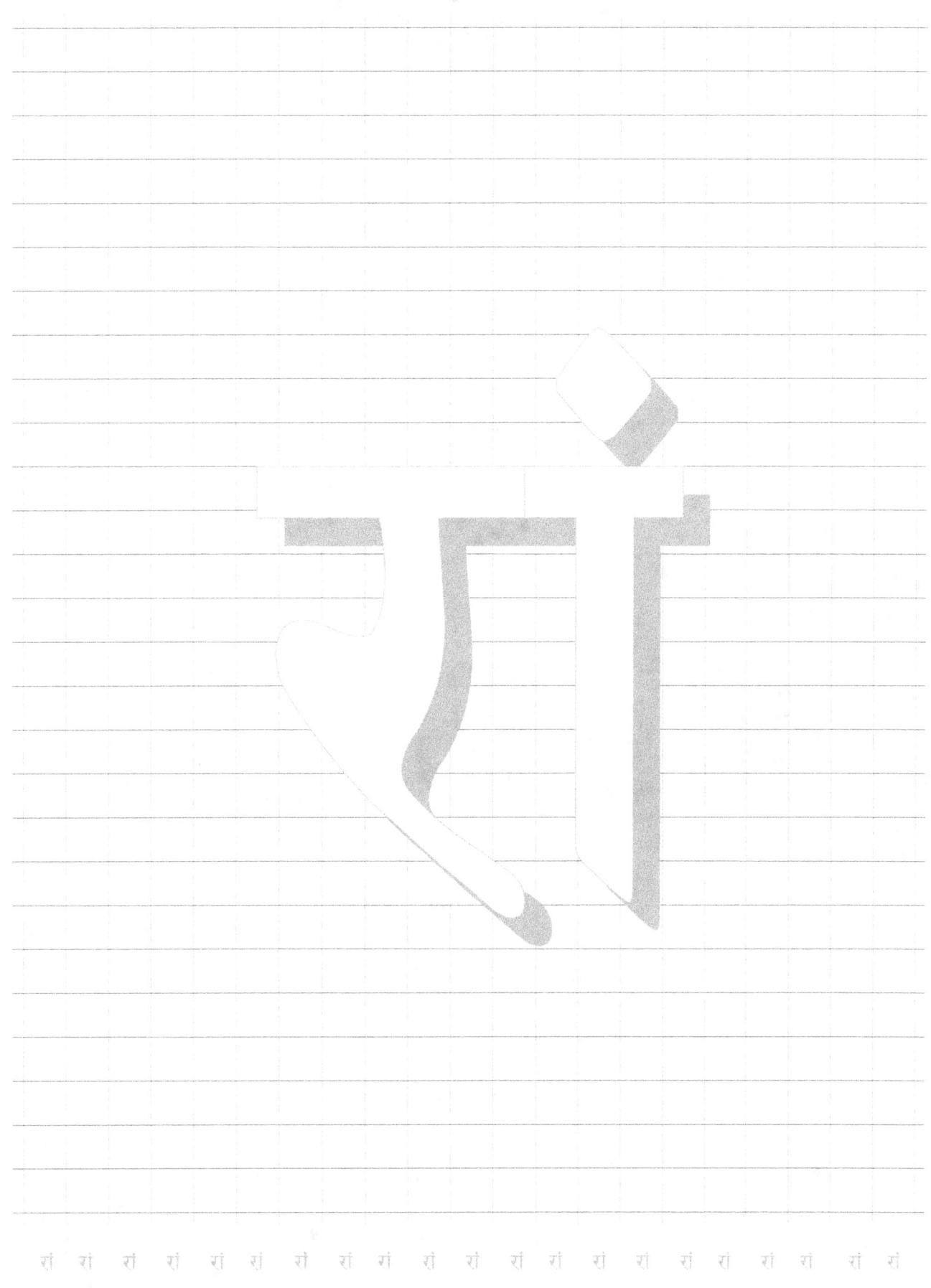

रों रों रों रों रों रों रों रों रों रों रों रों रों रों रों रों रों रों रों रों

16

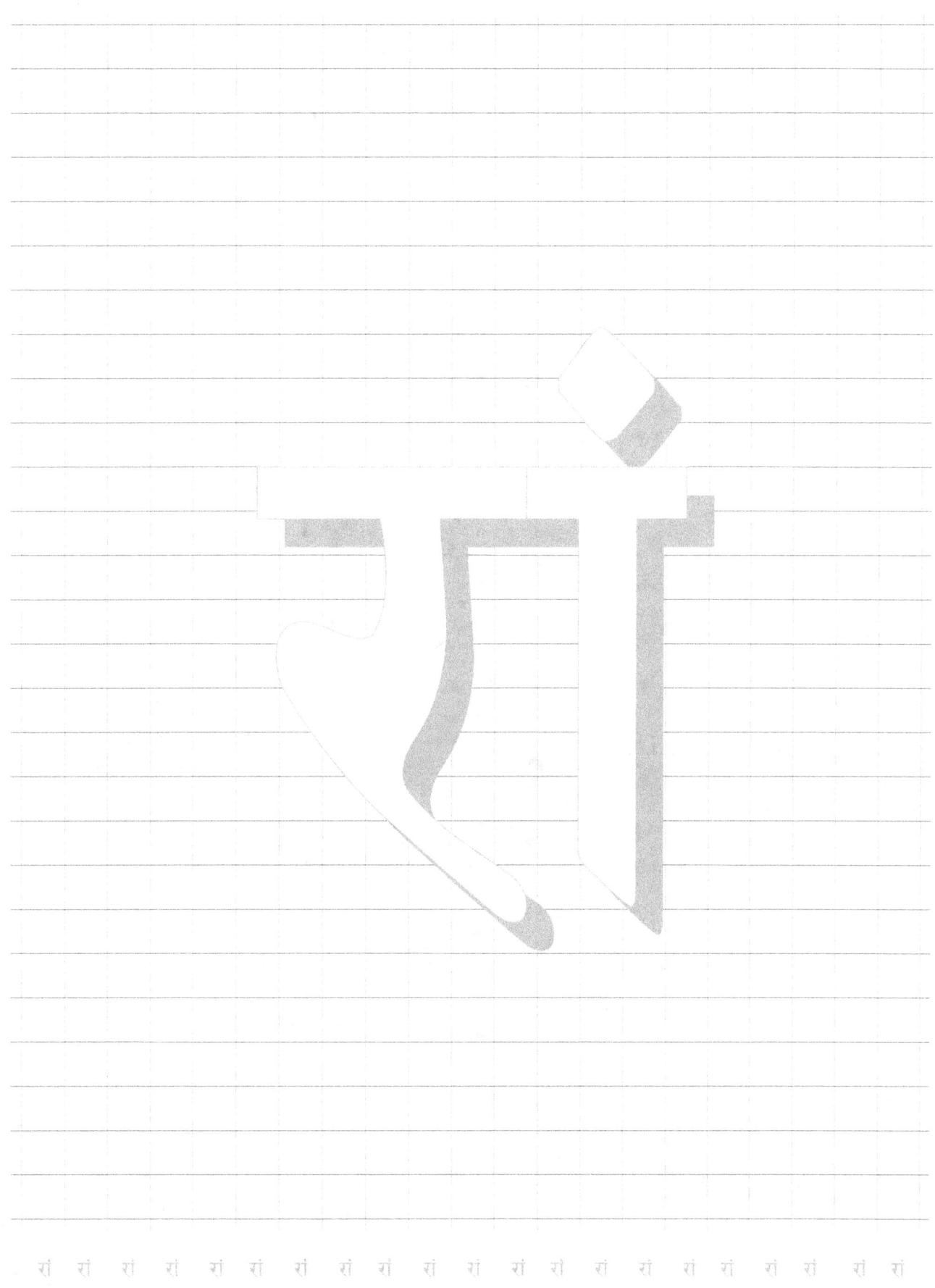

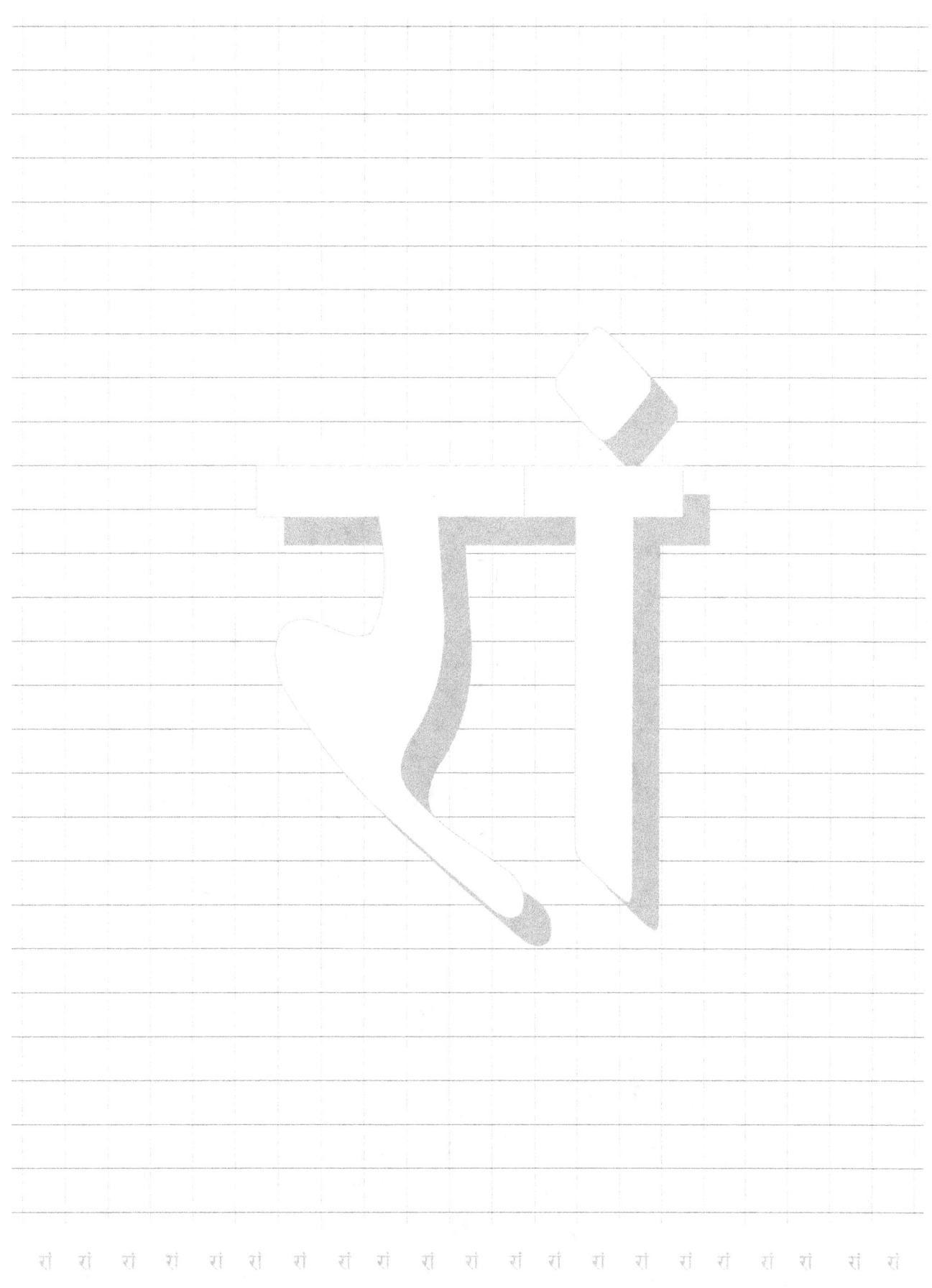

रां

रं रं

रां रां रां रां रां रां रां रां रां रां रां रां रां रां रां रां रां रां रां रां

रों रों रों रों रों रों रों रों रों रों रों रों रों रों रों रों रों रों रों

रों रों रों रों रों रों रों रों रों रों रों रों रों रों रों रों रों रों

रां रां रां रां रां रां रां रां रां रां रां रां रां रां रां रां रां रां रां रां

रां रां रां रां रां रां रां रां रां रां रां रां रां रां रां रां रां रां रां रां

रं रं रं रं रं रं रं रं रं रं रं रं रं रं रं रं रं रं रं रं

रां   रां   रां   रां   रां   रां   रां   रां   रां   रां   रां   रां   रां   रां   रां   रां   रां   रां   रां   रां

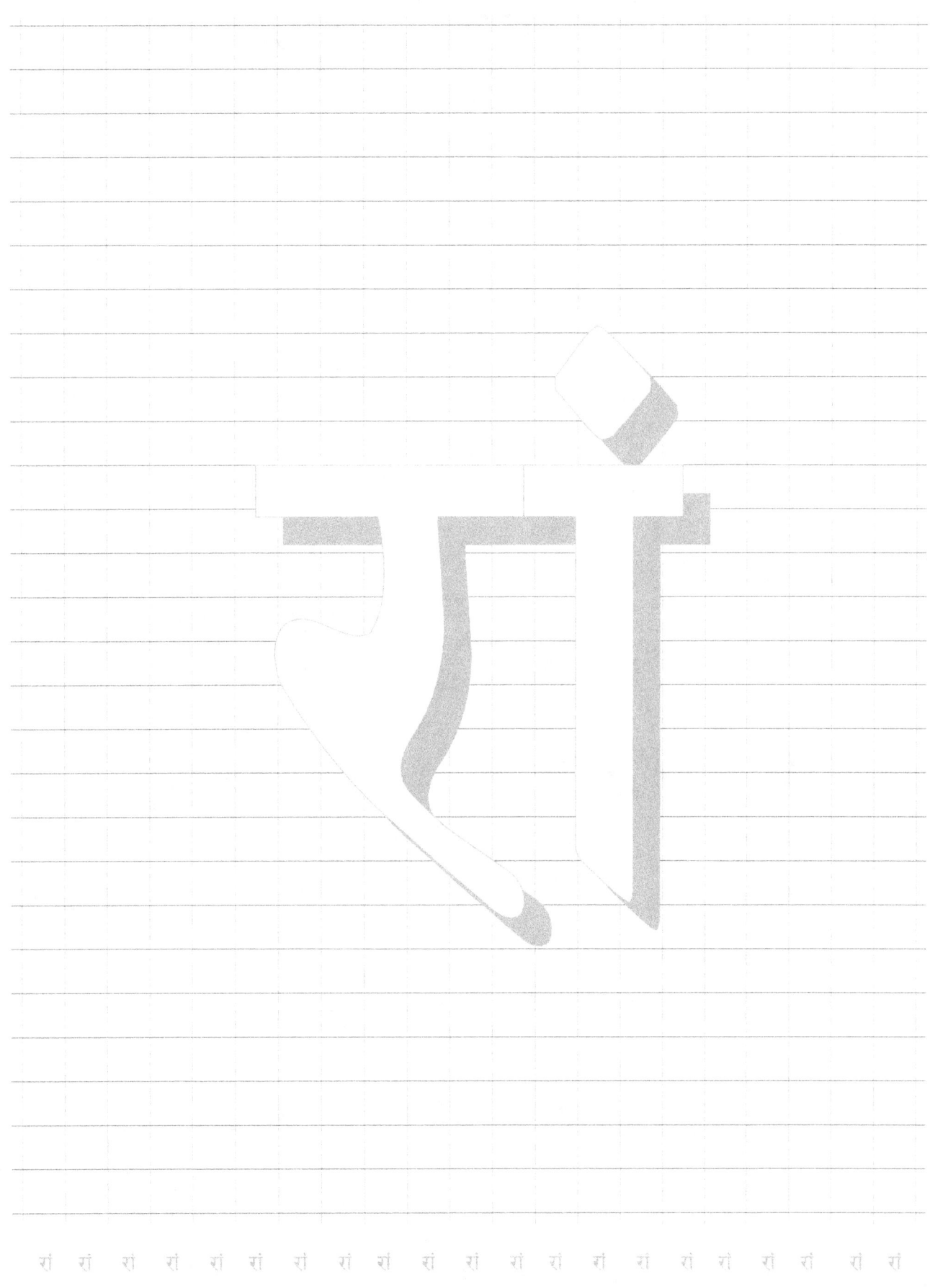

रों रों रों रों रों रों रों रों रों रों रों रों रों रों रों रों रों रों रों

रां रां रां रां रां रां रां रां रां रां रां रां रां रां रां रां रां रां रां

रां रां रां रां रां रां रां रां रां रां रां रां रां रां रां रां रां रां रां रां

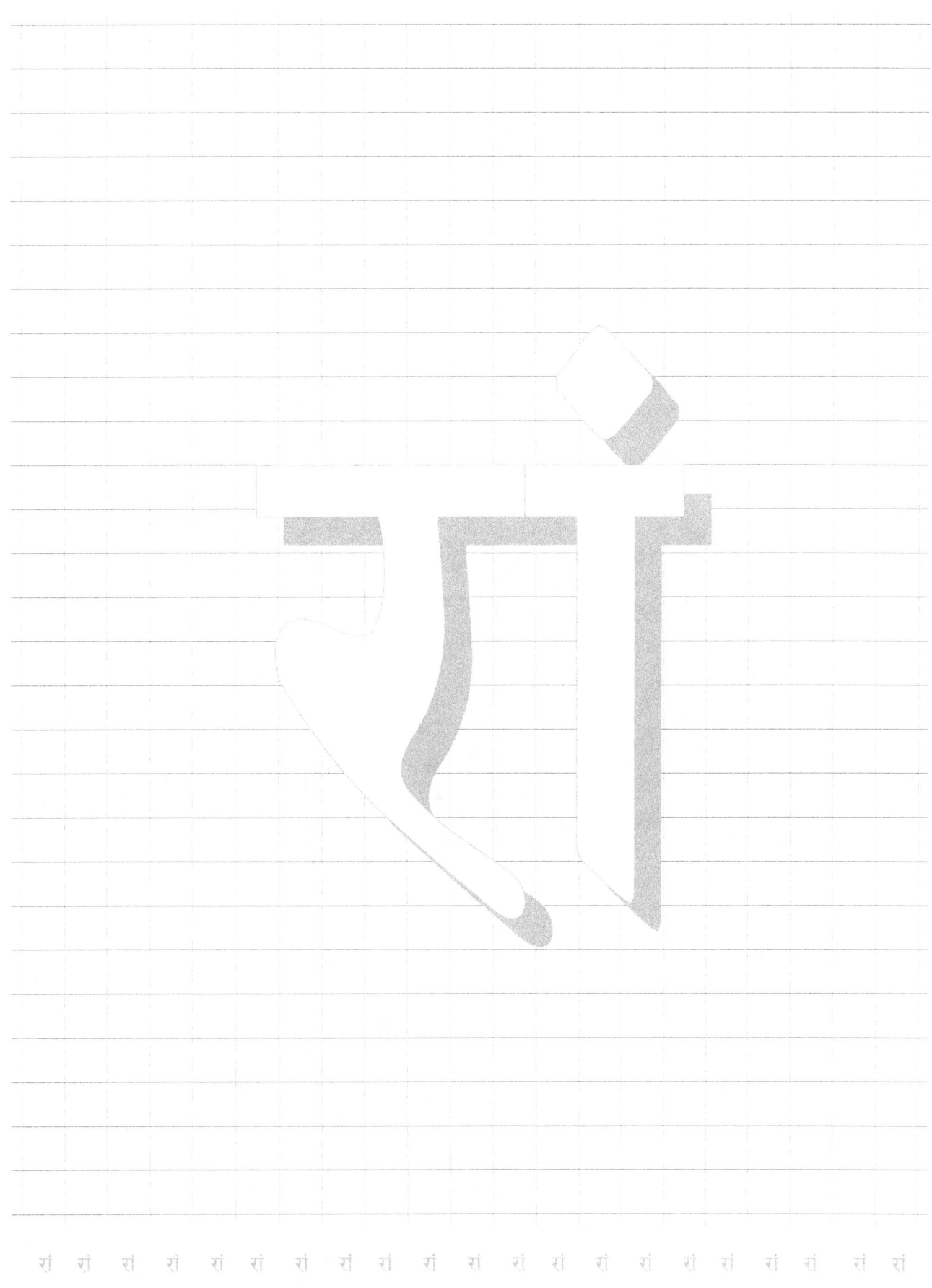

रां रां रां रां रां रां रां रां रां रां रां रां रां रां रां रां रां रां रां रां

रां रां रां रां रां रां रां रां रां रां रां रां रां रां रां रां रां रां रां रां

रां रां रां रां रां रां रां रां रां रां रां रां रां रां रां रां रां रां रां रां

रों रों रों रों रों रों रों रों रों रों रों रों रों रों रों रों रों रों रों रों

रों रों रों रों रों रों रों रों रों रों रों रों रों रों रों रों रों रों रों रों

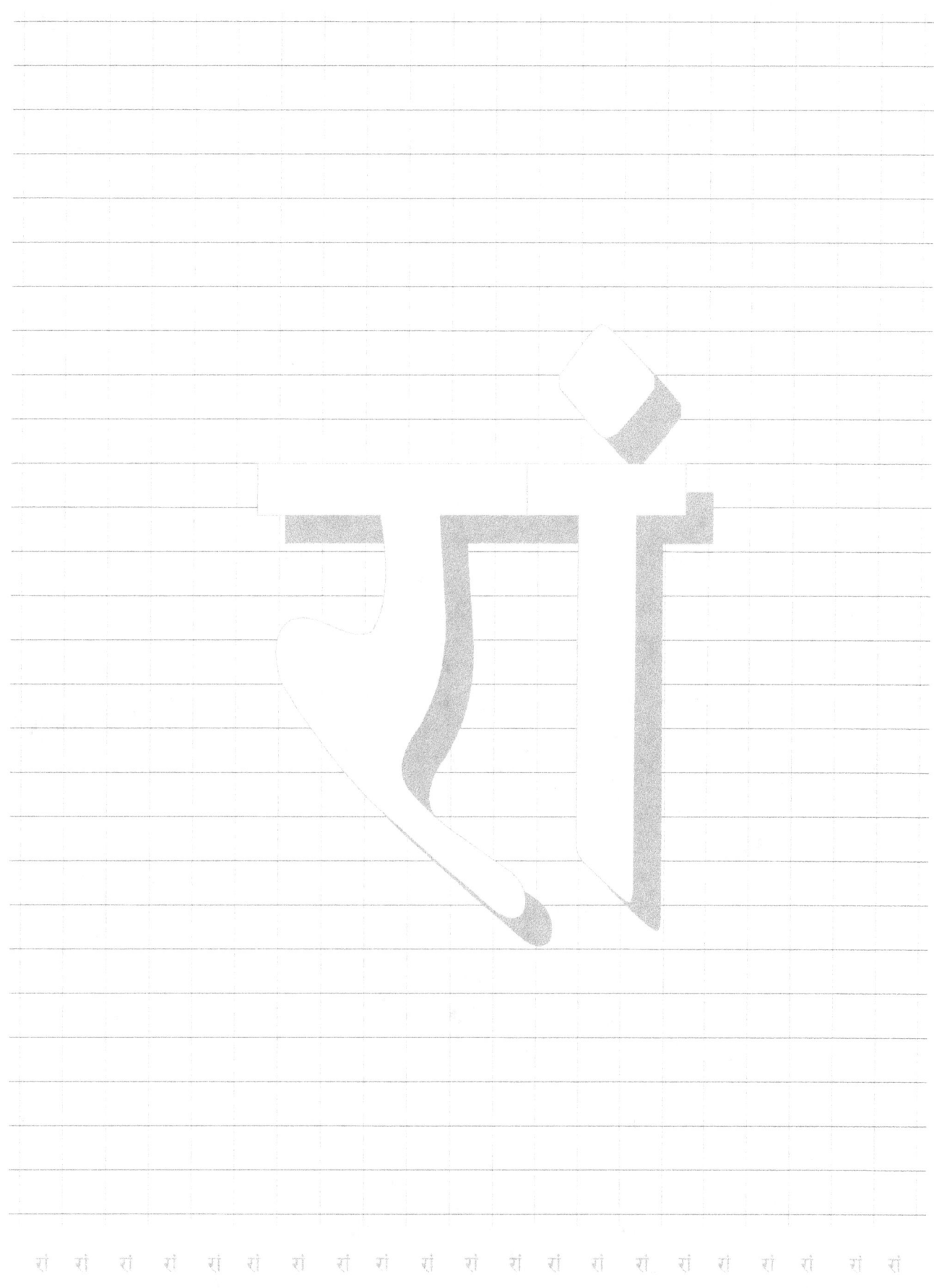

रां रां रां रां रां रां रां रां रां रां रां रां रां रां रां रां रां रां रां

रां रां रां रां रां रां रां रां रां रां रां रां रां रां रां रां रां रां

रां रां रां रां रां रां रां रां रां रां रां रां रां रां रां रां रां रां रां रां

54
_____ Today's Date

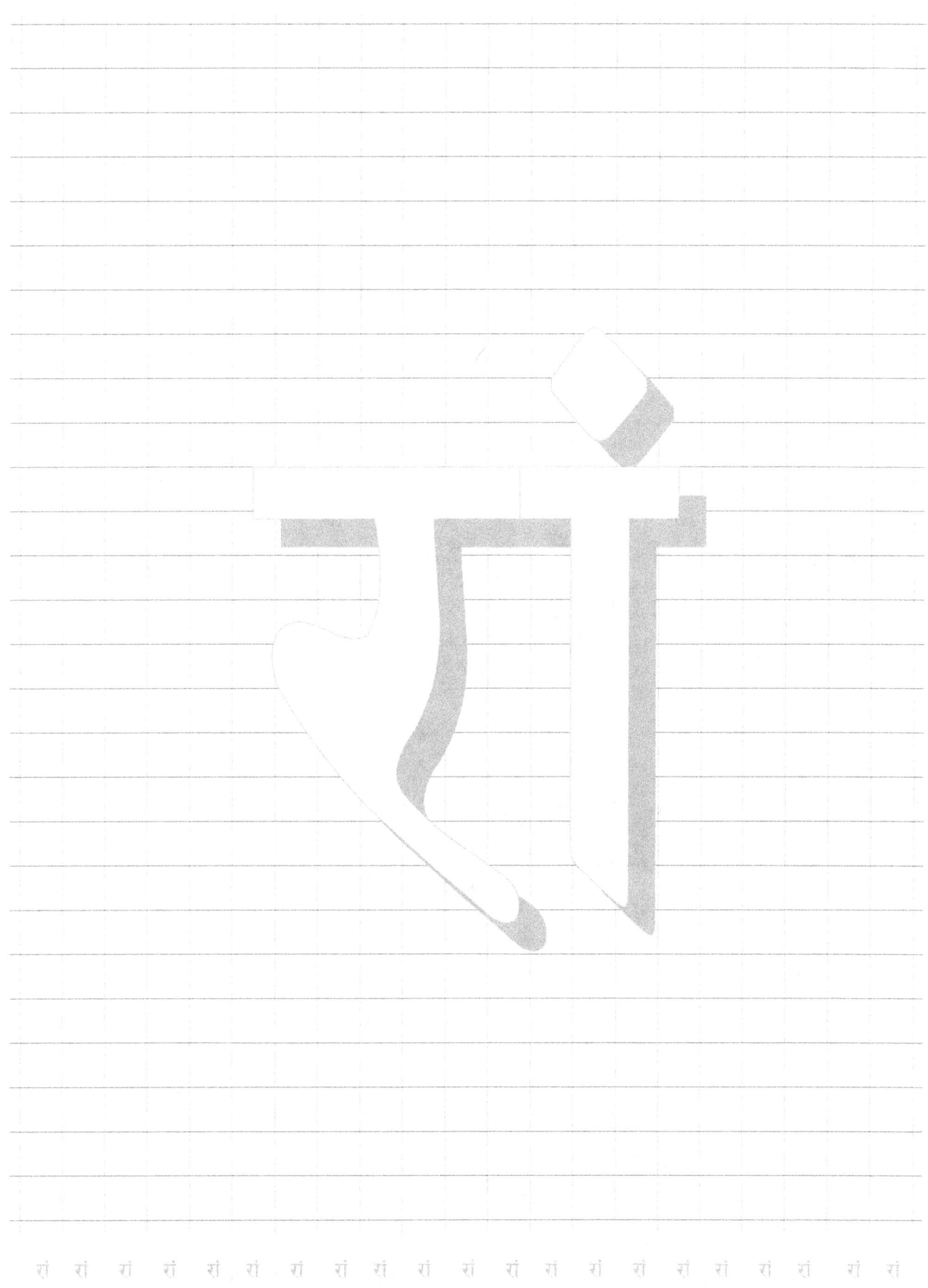

रां रां रां रां रां रां रां रां रां रां रां रां रां रां रां रां रां रां रां

रां रां

रों रों रों रों रों रों रों रों रों रों रों रों रों रों रों रों रों रों रों रों

रां रां रां रां रां रां रां रां रां रां रां रां रां रां रां रां रां रां रां रां

रां रां रां रां रां रां रां रां रां रां रां रां रां रां रां रां रां रां रां

रां

रों रों रों रों रों रों रों रों रों रों रों रों रों रों रों रों रों रों रों रों

रां रां रां रां रां रां रां रां रां रां रां रां रां रां रां रां रां रां रां रां

रां रां रां रां रां रां रां रां रां रां रां रां रां रां रां रां रां रां रां रां

रां रां रां रां रां रां रां रां रां रां रां रां रां रां रां रां रां रां रां

रां रां रां रां रां रां रां रां रां रां रां रां रां रां रां रां रां रां रां रां

रों रों रों रों रों रों रों रों रों रों रों रों रों रों रों रों रों रों रों रों

रों

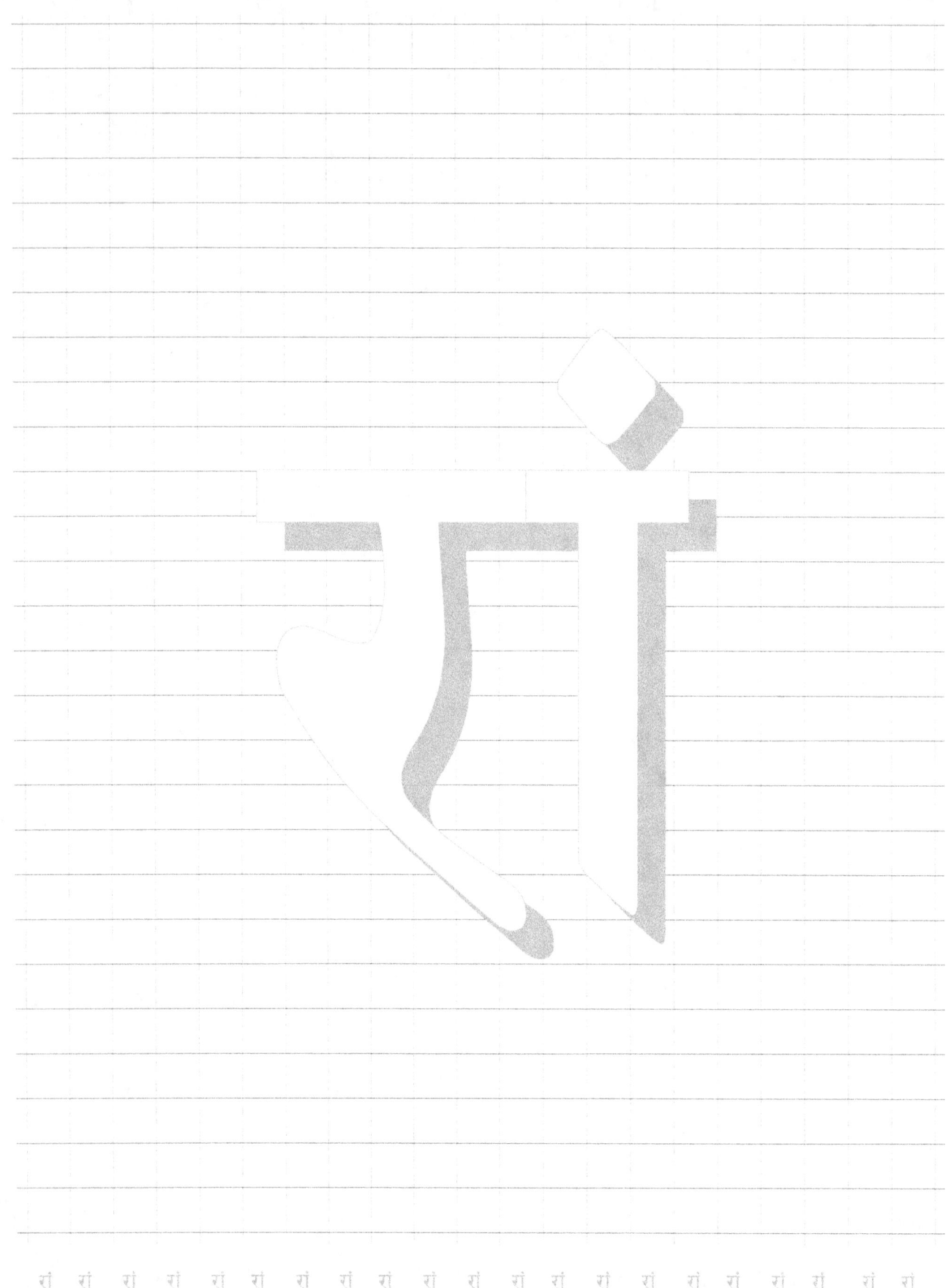

रां रां रां रां रां रां रां रां रां रां रां रां रां रां रां रां रां रां रां

रां रां रां रां रां रां रां रां रां रां रां रां रां रां रां रां रां रां रां रां

80 _____ Today's Date

रां रां रां रां रां रां रां रां रां रां रां रां रां रां रां रां रां रां रां रां

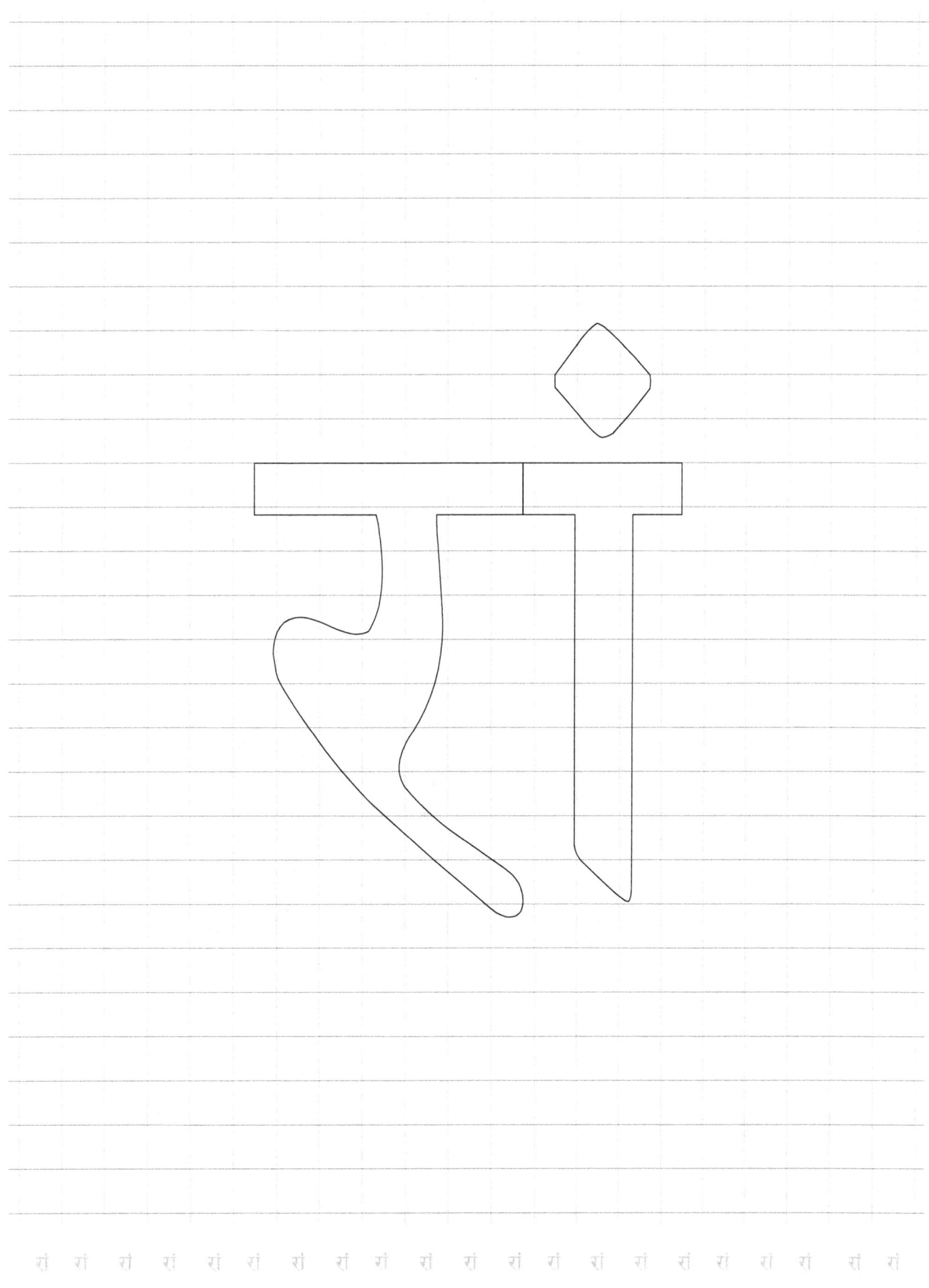

रां रां रां रां रां रां रां रां रां रां रां रां रां रां रां रां रां रां रां रां

रां रां

रां

रों रों रों रों रों रों रों रों रों रों रों रों रों रों रों रों रों रों रों रों

रां रां रां रां रां रां रां रां रां रां रां रां रां रां रां रां रां रां रां रां

रं रं रं रं रं रं रं रं रं रं रं रं रं रं रं रं रं रं रं रं

रों रों रों रों रों रों रों रों रों रों रों रों रों रों रों रों रों रों रों रों

रां रां

रां रां रां रां रां रां रां रां रां रां रां रां रां रां रां रां रां रां रां रां

रां रां रां रां रां रां रां रां रां रां रां रां रां रां रां रां रां रां रां रां

Today's Date : _____

97

रां रां

रं रं रं रं रं रं रं रं रं रं रं रं रं रं रं रं रं रं रं रं

रां रां रां रां रां रां रां रां रां रां रां रां रां रां रां रां रां रां रां रां

रां रां रां रां रां रां रां रां रां रां रां रां रां रां रां रां रां रां रां रां

रां रां रां रां रां रां रां रां रां रां रां रां रां रां रां रां रां रां रां

रां रां रां रां रां रां रां रां रां रां रां रां रां रां रां रां रां रां रां रां

www.ingramcontent.com/pod-product-compliance
Lightning Source LLC
Chambersburg PA
CBHW080026130526
44591CB00037B/2687